Bette & Joan

Anton Burge

A Samuel French Acting Edition

SAMUEL FRENCH
FOUNDED 1830

SAMUELFRENCH.COM
SAMUELFRENCH-LONDON.CO.UK

Copyright © 2014 by Anton Burge
All Rights Reserved
Cover image by

BETTE & JOAN is fully protected under the copyright laws of the United States of America, the British Commonwealth, including Canada, and all other countries of the Copyright Union. All rights, including professional and amateur stage productions, recitation, lecturing, public reading, motion picture, radio broadcasting, television and the rights of translation into foreign languages are strictly reserved.

ISBN 978-0-573-11053-5

www.SamuelFrench.com
www.SamuelFrench-London.co.uk

For Production Enquiries

United States and Canada
Info@SamuelFrench.com
1-866-598-8449

United Kingdom and Europe
Plays@SamuelFrench-London.co.uk
020-7255-4302

Each title is subject to availability from Samuel French, depending upon country of performance. Please be aware that *BETTE & JOAN* may not be licensed by Samuel French in your territory. Professional and amateur producers should contact the nearest Samuel French office or licensing partner to verify availability.

CAUTION: Professional and amateur producers are hereby warned that *BETTE & JOAN* is subject to a licensing fee. Publication of this play does not imply availability for performance. Both amateurs and professionals considering a production are strongly advised to the appropriate agent before starting rehearsals, advertising, or booking a theatre. A licensing fee must be paid whether the title is presented for charity or gain and whether or not admission is charged.

The professional rights in this play are controlled by Knight Hall Agency Ltd, Lower Ground Floor, 7 Mallow Street, London, EC1Y 8RQ

No one shall make any changes in this title for the purpose of production. No part of this book may be reproduced, stored in a retrieval system, or transmitted in any form, by any means, now known or yet to be invented, including mechanical, electronic, photocopying, recording, videotaping, or otherwise, without the prior written permission of the publisher. No one shall upload this title, or part of this title, to any social media websites.

MUSIC USE NOTE

Licensees are solely responsible for obtaining formal written permission from copyright owners to use copyrighted music in the performance of this play and are strongly cautioned to do so. If no such permission is obtained by the licensee, then the licensee must use only original music that the licensee owns and controls. Licensees are solely responsible and liable for all music clearances and shall indemnify the copyright owners of the play(s) and their licensing agent, Samuel French, against any costs, expenses, losses and liabilities arising from the use of music by licensees. Please contact the appropriate music licensing authority in your territory for the rights to any incidental music.

IMPORTANT BILLING AND CREDIT REQUIREMENTS

If you have obtained performance rights to this title, please refer to your licensing agreement for important billing and credit requirements.

BETTE AND JOAN was first produced by Ann Pinnington in association with Andy Jordan at the Arts Theatre, London, on 6th May 2011. The performance was directed by Bill Alexander and designed by Ruari Murchison. The cast was as follows:

BETTE DAVIS .... Greta Scacchi
JOAN CRAWFORD. .... Anita Dobson

CHARACTERS

BETTE DAVIS – Hollywood actress, 54. A star who has nothing to prove. Brisk, no nonsense, to the point of abruptness, caustic, brittle, difficult, vulnerable and funny. At the time of filming, a low point in her life and career. Has worked steadily through the '50s, though often with unrewarding results. Angry at the state of the business and her position within it. A professional to her fingertips. Four times married, recently divorced, mother of three (two adopted). All that matters now is the work.

JOAN CRAWFORD – Hollywood star, admits to 54, though is actually 58; as an actress has much to prove. Glamorous, neurotic, moody, vulnerable, generous and alcoholic. Desperate for approval. Comfortable playing the star, though there is always an uncertainty about this, stemming from a childhood that lacked education and love, from which she struggled, reinventing herself, to survive in the toughest of businesses. Four times married, recently widowed, mother of four (all adopted). Throughout her life, in spite of adversity, the image of Joan Crawford, star, continues to shine.

SCENE

The action of the play takes place in Hollywood during 1962.

A NOTE ON COSTUMES

BETTE: Day clothes should be blocks of colour: black was her most common choice, simple, tailored, unaffected, often cotton or linen.

A love of jewellery all antique, in particular charm bracelets. Also worn: broaches or broach pins, rings and a watch and pearls. Hair at the time of filming the famous outgrown page boy bob of 'All About Eve'.

Robe and dressing room attire, look to 'All About Eve' dressing room scene for inspiration.

JOAN: Immaculate, serviceable and matching. In pastel shades and often patterned in contrast to Bette's. Accessories all made in the same fabrics, including a hat, shoes covered with a film of plastic. Jewellery: a coordinating set of stones that would link with her outfit.

Robes: feminine and flowing, like gowns.

Hair can be the same as worn for Blanche.

JANE: Baby Jane Hudson gown, with pale blue sash. Look to the appropriate scene in the film.

BLANCHE: Has two distinct gowns in the film, one in red/rust and the other in blue: both deep, rich colours.

GENERAL NOTE: Colours should remain slightly muted to give the impression of grainy colourisation, as if of a black and white film that has been coloured. Some elements of the set could remain more black, white and grey.

MUSIC

Louis Prima: 'Sing, Sing, Sing' (Instrumental Version)

ANTON BURGE

Actor and writer Anton Burge has written eight plays for women, all focusing on the lives of celebrated women of the 19th and 20th centuries, including *Whatever Happened to the Cotton Dress Girl?*, *G & I* (both New End Theatre, Hampstead), *Storm in a Flower Vase*, (Arts Theatre) *Bette & Joan* (Arts Theatre, UK tour and a Broadway production planned for next year), and the forthcoming *Lady Mosley's Suite* and *Gung Ho Gertie!* He is also the author of a forthcoming book *Portraying Elizabeth*, a study of actresses' interpretations of Elizabeth I, from Sarah Bernhardt to the present day.

THANKS

The author would like to thank Ann Pinnington, Stephen Wicks, Emily Hayward, Deborah Smith, Bill Alexander, Greta Scacchi, Anita Dobson, Katie Langridge and Lucy Hume.

for Ann Pinnington

ACT ONE

(8:45 a.m. The Producers Studio, Melrose Avenue, Hollywood. Voices off: Technical, Wigs, Wardrobe staff etc: 'Good morning Miss Crawford'/Monty has left your lashes for you to choose, Miss Crawford'/'How are you today Miss Crawford?'/'Set up will be ready for Blanche's bedroom at ten'.)

(Lights up on a modest dressing room/trailer. A wheelchair for the character of Blanche, off centre. Dressing table, the mirror cut away, and chair centre stage, close to the adjoining wall of the other dressing room. All upholstered items covered in a layer of plastic. Also present: clothes rail, drinks cabinet and telephone.)

(All is spotless and clinical, the clothes on the rail wrapped in cellophane. Luxury is expressed by miscellaneous items such as a large amount of flowers, clothes and feminine accessories: perfume bottles, make-up etc. Pepsi Cola bottles are abundant. A fridge full of Pepsi bottles at the rear of the room. There are also piles of fan mail and photographs to be signed and scripts to read. **JOAN** *often refers to, and touches for assurance, a diary schedule.)*

(The overall visual effect is that of a monochrome, as in a black and white movie, which has been colourised, giving a period and slightly muted effect.)

(Across the other half of the stage a matching dressing room/trailer will be revealed, in reverse. A solitary gardenia plant is the only indication of opulence. A mirror image of the other dressing room, minus the wheelchair, an armchair in its place. Also a wig block upon which sits the Baby Jane Hudson wig. On the dressing table just the essentials and a thermos jug of

coffee, photographs of **BETTE**'s *family and dogs, cigarette boxes, cigarette containers (she had a particular fondness for china animal cigarette pots, often in the shape of chickens and cockerels), and ash trays are everywhere. Both stars have open, marked, worn scripts on the set at all times.)*

(The main mirrors, each attached to the dividing wall, are in fact suggested and is full length downstage, so that when **BETTE** *and* **JOAN** *come to look at their own reflections together, they are in fact looking at each other.)*

(Both rooms have director chairs, with their names embossed on the back, facing the audience as the curtain rises.)

(Lights up **JOAN CRAWFORD**'s *dressing room.* **JOAN**, *lying on the floor, knees raised, immaculately turned out in shorts and exercise blouse, her hair pristine covered by a lace net, practises deep breathing. Her eyes are concealed by an eye mask. Her heeled 'Pump Me' slippers remain on even when exercising. Each ensemble she wears matches.)*

(After a moment the telephone rings. She rises, removes the eye mask and composes herself, checks her perfect make-up, including rubber tyre lips, heavy eyebrows etc, dabs her brow with a chiffon handkerchief, and answers the telephone. When she speaks it is with careful, modulated tones. Like many alcoholics she perspires. Her movements are always poised, somewhat athletic, as if she is constantly on camera. She consults her watch.)

JOAN. Good morning, Patricia *(pronounced* Patreecia*)* and isn't it a beautiful morning... Thank you for my call, you were right on time... Yes, dear; yes I know the scene... Now would you mind telling them that I refuse to rehearse with anything but an empty plate. When the camera is ready to shoot the scene, and only then, they may bring the rodent in – I almost said animal – they look so big, but I believe it is a rodent, the rat? Would I be correct?... Bless you... No I'll be ready. Take one... Yes, that is what I said, take one and that will be the take Bob will print...

No, not at all...and while we are on the subject the temperature in my room isn't correct, it is far too hot... And make sure the set is the same... Oh, and remind Bob, no close-ups after four-thirty... Yes, dear, curfew... That will be all.

(She replaces the receiver. She then rises and puts on a long robe, accentuating her shoulders. In so doing she undoes her shorts and steps out of them, under the robe, leaving them on the floor.)

Wonderful to do these types of scenes, wonderful to be in front of the camera again, marvellous to feel the warmth of the lights. It's what I was born to do. The only thing I've ever truly known. It's my life and I'm so glad to be a part of this magical business. To show my fans I had the balls to return.

(She settles in the wheelchair.)

We did the dead canary scene yesterday. I had rehearsed with an empty plate, I always insist on that, and when the camera was ready I said 'You may bring on the platter'. But there was some kind of technical hitch; even so I kept my focus, kept the emotion (I don't think one should rehearse too much) and was very firm and said: 'Take the bird away'. Whatever had to be fixed was fixed, and when we came to shoot, take one, there it was, in the can!

Wonderful to be a perfectionist and that's what Joan Crawford is. She's a tough dame. She's got balls.

So exciting. I was telling Louella Parsons only yesterday – she's writing one of her beautiful articles about me – I said, 'Louella, I've always felt this way about making pictures. I want to bring the audience, my lovely fans, so close, that I have them in the palm of my hand. And when you go to a movie theatre, and find that you have done that, with a couple of scenes, well, as an artist, that's very rewarding. Very.'

I did rehearse a great deal with the wheelchair though, and my arms are as firm as a bat for it… I feel Blanche Hudson, movie star, the marvellous part I'm creating, and Joan Crawford, movie star, deserve it. I said to our director, Bob Aldrich, when we first discussed the role:

(JOAN rises and opens her robe wide, revealing her underwear – her blouse can be velcro-fastened to make the reveal one take with the robe.)

Take a look, Mr. Aldrich, take a good look. This is what you've got to work with. This is Joan Crawford and she's one hell of a star! *(A beat.* **JOAN** *finally closes her robe)* I do that with all my directors. It's one hell of an ice breaker.

(Sitting at her dressing table she picks up a big bundle of knitting.)

I'm loving playing Blanche Hudson, and Bette Davis, my co-star, well…well she's a very interesting personality, very.

The press, Hedda and Louella included, are trying to kick up the dust between us, so Bette gave a press release the other day: 'Getting along just fine, sorry, no feud!' So original.

Though I must admit I would prefer it if she refrained from telling the reporters that Joan Crawford is a very accomplished motion picture star, but *she*, Bette, is an actress!

(The sound of heels coming swiftly along the corridor. Voices off: 'Good morning Miss Davis', 'Page 72 Miss Davis', 'Hi Bette', 'The staircase scene, Bette, careful on the stairs'. **BETTE** *remains silent before exclaiming: 'Ha!' to a request.* **JOAN** *rises from the dressing table and goes to the door.)*

JOAN. *(at the doorway, to* **BETTE***)* Good morning, Bette, dear. And how are you today?

BETTE. *(ignores her. Entering)* Oh shit. Good manners.

JOAN. *(to herself)* Yes, sir! Getting along fine, sorry, no feud! *(***JOAN*** slams the door and goes back to her knitting. Cross-fade to* **BETTE***'s dressing room.* **BETTE** *slams her door behind her)*

BETTE. They don't have to damn well tell me about playing scenes on stairs. Spent half my life goin' up 'em, the other comin' down. Christ!

They think just because I've been in the business two hundred years, and have something of a reputation, I'm gonna fall on my ass, break my back again and file an insurance claim!

(The telephone rings.)

Jesus! It's the kids of today who do that, *not* the professionals. *(Into the receiver)* Yep. Sure, I know, they just told me.

(She replaces the receiver, cutting the other voice off. Begins to get ready for the day's shooting. She doesn't waste a second, is rarely still, a mass of energy. In time she will smoke and drink a cup of coffee from the thermos jug on her dressing table.)

Don't they remember I was at Warner Bros. Studios, this very studio, for eighteen years, till those sons of bitches decided Battling Bette was too expensive a commodity? Not that I evah got what the male stars got. Oh boy, no! But then why would I? I'm a female!

(The telephone rings again, interrupting her preparations.)

Gonna rip that sucker out the wall one of these days! *(Into the receiver) Well?*... Has it turned up then? Just let me know when it does. Said it damn well should have been here by now.

(She bangs the receiver back onto the telephone. Continues to get ready)

But when it comes to staircases don't tell me to be careful!

Christ, if I'd been careful, wouldn't have had the career I've had. *Jezebel* (pronounced *'Jezeble'*), *Dark Victory*, *Little Foxes*, they all had sets dominated by staircases, *All About Eve*'s 'bumpy night!' on a staircase. Why, in *The Letter*, the picture opened on stairs, and was frankly, god damn it, *the* greatest opening sequence *evah* played on film, no question about it!

(She rises, mid preparation, caught up in the memory, and in time acts out the scene, reliving her former triumph. The lighting changes, closing in about her to give the effect of the 1940 melodrama. The sound of a projector running.)

The credits roll. The Malay moon shines down on the sleeping rubber plantation of Robert Crosbie. The rubber drips, the servant boys drowse… All is silent. Quiet as the grave.

Suddenly a shot rings out, a bird flies out of the jungle, then another shot and another and Mrs. Crosbie – me – follows a stumbling man from the bungalow, down the veranda steps, emptying a barrel-load of bullets into him.

We hear the click of the last report, the dust begins to settle and the moon emerges from behind a cloud. Close up on me as I stare at it; widen eyes as if guided by it. *Genius!*

(The light reverts to the set once again and colour washes over her. She returns to the dressing table.)

The *(often pronounced 'thee')* greatest opening of any picture, before or since, no question about it.
And they tell me to be careful! Huh!

(Lights up on **JOAN** *as* **BETTE** *removes her clothes, down to her petticoat, and puts on a plain white robe and slippers; the look reminiscent of Margo Channing in 'All About Eve'. Both sit at their dressing tables.* **JOAN** *adds finishing touches to her make-up and also lotion to her skin. In time she will also apply scent from an atomiser.* **BETTE**, *pinning up her hair, removes her day make-up with cold cream, before applying the full Jane hag mask.)*

JOAN. Always the same, every day, nine a.m. on the dot. Never 'Hello' or 'Good morning' to anyone. So rude.

Whereas I love a warm welcome whenever I enter a studio, even here in a part of Warner Bros. that I never came to before, where the 'B' pictures were churned out, even here. For Joan Crawford, every morning on any film set is a homecoming.

She's always been very difficult. I've always believed, though golly I would never say, it was due to a disorganised sex life. I can't think why more people haven't picked up on it. You've only to look at her to see that.

BETTE. *(looking at her figure before closing her robe)* Sex is usually such a bad bet; at least that has always been my experience.

Ha! Said that to her the other day. *(Nodding towards* **JOAN**'s *dressing room)*

JOAN. She said, 'Sex is such a bad bet'.

BETTE. In a moment of weakness. To which she replied:

JOAN. I said, 'Gambling can be so bad for the figure, Bette dear!'

BETTE. I could have punched her in the fucking face!

JOAN. I knew she was a handful: a loose cannon. When I was first introduced to her I was just about to marry my second husband, the stage actor Franchot Tone. They were making a picture together – *Dangerous*, I think it was called – some turgid little pot boiler, that didn't really get any recognition…

BETTE. Won my first Oscar for a little picture called *Dangerous*.

JOAN. …and Bette, a perfectionist even back then it seems, was always wanting to rehearse in the evenings; all eyes and talent!

BETTE. *Dangerous* wasn't a great script, but I knew I could make it into something. Franchot Tone was swell – screwed everything that moved, but a great actor nonetheless.

JOAN. I did eventually become *Mrs* Franchot Tone, though their squalid little affair left a bitter memory, from which our marriage never truly recovered. In time we both knew when it was over…and it was over.

(A short beat. Then more brightly)

Of course I insisted on remaining friends. I do that with all my ex-husbands. When they leave I change the locks and the toilet seats, but they'll always have a place in my heart.

BETTE. That bitch wouldn't let him out of her sight! Always hanging around the set, slowing things down with picnic baskets, afternoon tea and her fucking knitting. I remember thinking at the time: 'If I'm as desperate as her when I reach that age, I'll, I'll…shoot myself!'

JOAN. For some reason Bette likes to presume that I am older than she is. Check my birth certificate dear… *(Under her breath)* if you can lay your hands on one!

BETTE. Even when we'd wrapped she wouldn't let up. I even remember her taking a swipe at me for my choice of outfit the night I won my Oscar for *Dangerous*.

JOAN. Oscar night, 1936, Bette wore…well, I think it could only be described as…well, well…a bath robe. She was young back then – hard to believe, I know – with so much to learn about the industry. Labouring over her image as a working actress – we're all that, dear – but she has to remember that glamour is part of the business as well.

BETTE. I was even cornered in the ladies' room by a reporter, furious about it! She told me to start dressing and behaving like a star!

JOAN. Of course it was very different when I won my Oscar a few years later...

BETTE. Maybe I should have behaved like that clothes horse next door, feigned illness and received my award in bed. Not the first Oscar to hit her sheets I'm sure! Only to rise from the grave when she heard the announcement on the radio and the pop of a flashbulb outside!

JOAN. Even when close to death, one should always resemble a star.

BETTE. There was nothing wrong with her and nothing wrong with the outfit I wore in '36. I felt it was very fitting for a working actress.

Sylvia, that was the bitch reporter's name, informed her readers that she didn't like the parts I was fighting so hard to play: the girls with guts, the wicked ladies, the bitches, the tragic heroines: the *real* women, never seen on screen before.

JOAN. Winning the Oscar for *Mildred Pierce* meant so much to me. Not only was I accepted by my fans, but by my peers and the press as well. One journalist, Sylvia, used to write a beautiful column called 'Advice to the Stars!' She would always say 'Of course, Joan, you're the one star in Hollywood I never have to give advice to!'

BETTE. *(at the wig block, smoking)* wonder what Sylvia would make of Baby Jane?

A lot of people in the know begged me not to take this part, but I've got an inkling... Miss Crawford has too... something good's gonna come of this picture.

JOAN. This picture will put Joan Crawford right back on top!

(A beat. Joan settles into the wheelchair) Though I must admit I've never made anything quite like this before! Our director Bob Aldrich loves such evil subjects, vile,

horrendous things; so dark. An aging, psychotic child star terrorises her beautiful and glamorous movie star sister in a creepy gothic mansion full of shadows and secrets. This isn't really my type of brand, it's much more Bette's line.

BETTE. I'll give the critics a field day, I do know that! Directors in the past have often said to me: 'Now Bette, are you sure you want to go before the camera looking like that?' But my fans love it. They love to see me go out on a limb, and after all it's only looking as the character would look – isn't that what acting is all about?

JOAN. I mean I could never do that to myself, what Bette is doing, just plying on the greasepaint for effect, or do it to my public for that matter! Of course she's always been happy to make herself a grotesque...though a little bird did tell me she sat in the screening room last night and wept till her mascara ran.

BETTE. *Hell,* what am I supposed to do, work every fifteen years like Claudette Colbert?

Thank God I love it as I do, Christ, you've got to love it, love, *love* making pictures. At least that hasn't altered.

(Cross-fade to **JOAN** *picking up the telephone receiver)*

JOAN. Hello, who is this please?... Ah, hello there... *(More briskly)* Tell Mamacita be ready in 45 minutes to go on the set...bless you.

(Replaces the receiver, rises and continues exercising)

Mamacita, my maid. She's been with me for years. Never says very much, but then I don't want confidences. I want someone who, when I say, 'Have the coral suit with the long skirt, pressed and ready for me', boy, is she ready!

She's a very gifted packer, for travelling, Pepsi Cola functions, or filming on location. She realizes Joan Crawford has to damn well look her best for her fans, and she makes damn sure that I do.

Those wonderful, charming fans. Without them Joan Crawford wouldn't exist and I'd be back in the dirt of Kansas City. Some fans call me up—

BETTE. *(applying the chalky pancake make-up at her dressing table)* Much as I love making pictures, I certainly wouldn't give my fans my telephone number like somebody I could mention.

JOAN. Really, some fans call me—

BETTE. She actually gives her fans her telephone number! Jesus!

JOAN. And I *love* that. One called only yesterday, just to hear my voice, and to ask what I was wearing. *(Moved)* Such a beautiful, enchanting gesture...

When they stop on the sidewalk and say, 'Why look, there's Joan Crawford!' I reply, 'Why yes it is!', blow them a kiss and ask, 'And how are you today?' I owe that to them, *and* to always look my best. I never leave the house unless I look like Joan Crawford.

BETTE. She once said to me, 'I never leave the house unless I look like Joan Crawford!' *(Chuckles)*

JOAN. I made the mistake of saying that to Bette recently. I was trying to be civil, golly how I try, but since we've started shooting...well, let's just say someone's manners have been allowed to slide.

(BETTE rises from the dressing table before studying her script, centre.)

BETTE. Well, who the fuck does she expect to leave the house as then!

JOAN. She's so coarse. My motto has always been, 'If you want to see the girl next door, go next door!' And who wants that?

(Exercising) Every morning I say to myself, 'Treasure yourself. Thank you, God, for making me a flier and not pedestrian. Thank you for this lovely day; now what can I contribute to it?'

I believe that is wonderful advice. For me that means remaining vital, gorgeous and sexy. Oh, sex is very important, it keeps a woman looking young as well. I'm very proactive when it comes to sex. Learn from your lovers and move on! As my stardom grew I learnt from the best: Spencer Tracy, Jeff Chandler, Rock Hudson, yes even Rock. Ah. *(A beat as she reminisces)* Jackie Cooper, Cesar Romero, Greg Bautzer. Ah. *(A beat as she reminiscences)* Douglas Fairbanks Junior, Vincent Sherman, Douglas Fairbanks Senior (just kidding!) and Yul Bryner: boy, what a king!

(Coming to her senses, returning to her seat) But for me the *real* King, oh my, *the* King: *Gable*. Gable every time. He was everything you would think him to be and more. Man at his most primeval, virile. The instincts of a wild beast. He had balls. It was a volcanic attraction we had for each other, a fire that only death could quench. He told our boss at MGM, Louis B. Mayer, that he wanted to divorce his wife and marry me. Papa Mayer, as we all called him, said, 'Marry that tramp Crawford? The daughter of a washer woman!' Gable had balls. But we never married, though no one but him would have stood up to Mr. Mayer like that.

(Sincerely) We loved each other right up until the end, through all our subsequent marriages: twenty-eight years, twenty-eight years of love. He taught me so much. He even understood my need to clean, knew that I had to have order and everything spotless. Like me he travelled with cleaning materials. He'd had an upbringing that he too wanted to wash away. I understood that. He had discipline. We both believed in it. Discipline in all you do.

BETTE. *(in dim relief)* The key to a female's success in this town is to simply be better! I can pick a decent script, never a decent man!

(JOAN *picks up the receiver again, a handkerchief dabbing her brow.*)

JOAN. Oh my. (*Into the receiver*) Patricia, Patricia, the temperature in my room hasn't been fixed, what seems to be the problem? ... It has? It can't have, dear... And the set, what temperature is that at now?... It should be at the level stated in my contract, always... And if it isn't, Patricia, you'll never work in Hollywood again... Thank you, dear, bless you. Love and eternal thanks.

(*She replaces the receiver and takes a slug of Pepsi. Lights fade up full on* BETTE, *make-up almost complete, hair still tied back, as she rises with her script and cigarette and exits her dressing room. Over the next segment of dialogue* JOAN *becomes angry and distressed, unravelling somewhat. This new* JOAN, *at odds with the sophisticated star we met initially, dons gloves and begins to clean her dressing room.*)

Such a pity standards have been allowed to slip in Hollywood. This would never have happened at MGM. Hollywood is fast becoming such a depressing place. I'm grateful, the most grateful human being in the world for what it has given me. It's given me my education, the power to adopt four beautiful children, to raise them, educate them. Hollywood has given me everything I ever owned; I will never be ungrateful to it for that. But now, oh my, you may *have it*. Where are the beautiful people, the moguls, the fathers to take care of us and guide us...the glamour, the *stars*—

(*A brief knock at the door.* BETTE *walks briskly in smoking a cigarette.*)

Come in... Oh hello, Bette. How can I...

BETTE. The running order has been changed.

JOAN. (*alert*) What do you mean?

BETTE. So we need to rehearse the lift—

JOAN. *(holding up her hand to silence* BETTE*)* It can't have been changed. I would have been told. Won't you sit down? *(She gestures towards the wheelchair.)*

BETTE. *(ignoring the offer)* Well it has, so we have to go over the lift again before Jane and Blanche head for the beach.

JOAN. But I don't understand. Bob was blocking for the rodent under the tureen scene last night, to shoot this morning. I've been preparing—

BETTE. Well, we talked last night, he and I, and it just made more sense to shoot it this way round and do the rat tomorrow.

(JOAN *tenses.)*

They're nearly ready for us out there.

JOAN. But I haven't prepared.

BETTE. *(ignoring her, waving her hand in the direction of* JOAN*'s face)* And you'll have to calm all that make-up down.

JOAN. *(picking up the telephone receiver)* Well, that's rich, I must say…

BETTE. Who are you calling? I want to rehearse the lift before we shoot it! We don't have time—

JOAN. Why, Bob of course. I need to speak to him, to run through my thoughts, my emotions and—

BETTE. You don't have anything to say in the scene!

JOAN. *(trying to be civil but politely snapping, the receiver still in her grasp)* I understand what you want, but I'm not really happy about this, Bette, dear. Whether I have a line or not makes no difference. This isn't the first time schedules have been altered after one of your late night chats with *our* director.

BETTE. *(ploughing on)* Now when I lift you, remember what I said and move with me, don't become a lump of lead, or I'll *nevah* shift ya!

JOAN. I should have been informed!

BETTE. *(enjoying the situation)* OK, no need to get hysterical.

JOAN. It's no wonder I can never get hold of Bob in the evening! And yes I do know about your condition. We've been through this, *several times*: because you broke your back a few years ago you—

BETTE. – I gotta be careful, so you need to help me on this one.

JOAN. But that still doesn't alter the fact that—

BETTE. Oh shit! I forgot to say good morning, didn't I? *Good morning.*

JOAN. *(a tight, momentary smile)* Good morning, Bette. Now I really am going to have to speak to Bob.

BETTE. He's on the set, wrapped in a sweater; it's a goddamn igloo out there. Call him if you must, if you think it will make a difference.

JOAN. Of course it will make a difference! It's both of our names up there above the title, you know. I think you forget that sometimes.

BETTE. And for Chrissake don't play the scene like you're Little Bo Peep!

*(***JOAN*** then notices ***BETTE****'s cigarette has almost burned down. Their eyes meet momentarily.)*

(After an embarrassing silence) I suppose you don't happen to have an ash tray?

*(***JOAN*** shakes her head looking at the offending article)*
A saucer?

*(***JOAN*** looks at ***BETTE*** incredulously)*
Well... *(***BETTE*** looks at the floor as a possible solution for stubbing out the cigarette)* Shit! I'll be back in a moment.

*(***BETTE*** exits and enters her dressing room fuming. She stubs out the cigarette and immediately lights another to calm herself, pacing the floor as ***JOAN***, infuriated that the order of her day has been upset, picks up the telephone receiver. Lights change, to imitate black and white, the sound of a projector runs and the atmosphere,*

lighting, music etc. take on a heightened filmic moment, as from 'Whatever Happened to Baby Jane?')

JOAN. Patricia, Patricia?... Yes it is important. I need your help. Is Mr. Aldrich there? I need to talk to him!... But I have to talk to him; you'll have to put him on, immediately... *(She waits nervously, anticipating* **BETTE***'s return.) Bob!*

BETTE. *(beginning to hear* **JOAN***'s raised voice)* Son of a bitch!

JOAN. Bob! Bob!... But I need to speak to him!, I need him here!... Yes, the way she is behaving... I need him here! Tell him immediately!

(In the meantime **BETTE** *has stubbed out her cigarette and exited her dressing room. Hearing part of the conversation outside* **JOAN***'s door she opens the door momentarily, unbeknownst to* **JOAN**, *and then lets it swing shut again.)*

(Working herself up) She's unbalanced... Yes! Yes, she is!... Thank you. Get him to come to Miss Crawford's dressing room as soon as you find him.

*(***BETTE** *re-enters her dressing room and picks up the telephone receiver aggressively.)*

BETTE. Bob Aldrich, and make it snappy... *(Calmly)* Bob, yes I know. I'm here with Joan... Well, you don't have to bother rushing along here now; we've sorted the problem out... Yes it is all taken care of... yea, so we'll see you on the set... yes, yes she's fine. See you in a while. *(She replaces the receiver, menacingly, using her 'Baby Jane' voice)* Goodbye director!

(Laughing outrageously as Baby Jane she exits. The lighting, music etc. reverts back. During this time, **JOAN**, *with the help of Pepsi and the knowledge that Bob will be along soon, has composed herself.* **BETTE** *knocks and enters.)*

JOAN. Ah, there you are, Bette. I've been in touch with Bob and he agrees we need to make these decisions together.

BETTE. Oh really? I agree; I'm sure it is for the best.

JOAN. *(exerting some control)* Now, when we shoot the tablet business, Jane will just hand the bottle to Blanche won't she? You won't actually...

BETTE. Touch the pill?

(JOAN nods and BETTE rolls her eyes.) I promise.

JOAN. I've had Mamacita sterilise the mouth tape, if you could be careful not to... *(She gestures towards her made-up lips. BETTE remains silent.)* You understand?

BETTE. Yeah.

JOAN. *(glancing at her watch)* So...

BETTE. Expecting someone?

(A beat)

JOAN. *(innocently)* No. *(Playing for time)* So what do you think of my Mr. Aldrich?

BETTE. Well, he's no Willie Wyler that's for sure.

JOAN. This is a marvellous opportunity for both of us. I hope you realise that, Bette.

BETTE. *(muttering)* A gig's a fucking gig.

JOAN. And Bob is a very celebrated director, very celebrated indeed.

BETTE. I'd hardly call *Sodom and Gomorrah* a celebrated picture!

JOAN. *(ignoring BETTE)* Of course, Bob and I have collaborated before.

BETTE. Oh, I'm sorry, were you in that?

JOAN. *(not amused. Looking at her watch)* Really.

BETTE. I think we can trust him to know what he's doing. *I* always think it's better to let directors get on with it, no question about it...

JOAN. If only *that* were true.

BETTE. Well, we both know what we've gotten ourselves into; it's hardly a remake of *Little Women*.

Now, Blanche is in bed tied up...

JOAN. *(a beat and another glance at her watch)* Oh, very well.

*(***JOAN** *rises and seats herself in the wheelchair with her hands raised above her head as if tied up.)*
Like so?

*(***BETTE** *acts out untying* **JOAN***'s hands and proceeds to drag her, hands clasped under* **JOAN***'s bust, across the floor to the door. The process comprises a false start.* **BETTE** *does the untying motion again, identically, and they finish the action.* **JOAN** *picks herself up off the floor.* **BETTE** *casually gives her a hand to help; it is refused)*

BETTE. Just don't become a lump a' lead, that's all.

JOAN. Thank you, dear, I have no intention.

BETTE. Well, don't forget.

JOAN. And don't drop me!

BETTE. *(heading for the door)* Oh brother.

JOAN. *(a beat, savouring this moment. She swallows some Pepsi)* Oh, before you go, Bette dear, will you be viewing the rushes tonight? I thought we could maybe sit together.

BETTE. I nevah go to the rushes, you know that. Every goddamn take I make is worth printing!

JOAN. Oh? I'd heard you went the other night?

BETTE. *(pausing at the door, sniffing danger)* What?

JOAN. It's incredible, I would have thought – *(Gesturing at* **BETTE***'s unkempt appearance)* I mean this being such a departure from your normal beautiful self: letting yourself go like this, I would have thought you'd have wanted to see what was happening. I know I would. *(On reflection, gaily laughing)* Not that I could ever do what you're do—

BETTE. *(at the door. Tightly)* Oh, I just remembered. I think Bob wants to shoot the *kicking* sequence later – did he tell you? Or perhaps there wasn't time to see you this morning?

JOAN. *(reverting to her former mood, working herself up)* Well, I would have thought that was obvious. No, of course he hasn't told me. *(Dabbing her forehead)* I had hoped... *(Beginning to realise he has let her down)* He should understand all these changes upset me. I know we are limited for time—

BETTE. – You're damn right there!

JOAN. – but I can't really believe he would do this; we have a history, he and I. I believed in him, still believe in him, but he needs to make changes with gentleness, with kindness.

BETTE. *(ignoring her, going for the kill)* Also there is a cut on page eighty-nine.

JOAN. A cut? *(She hurriedly flicks though her script)*

BETTE. Yea, I hope you don't mind. It holds me up.

JOAN. *(sipping Pepsi nervously)* I'll have to look at it... it, it just gets me so jumpy, filming at this, this...

BETTE. Pace.

JOAN. Thank you, Bette, yes, pace.

BETTE. As I said, we both know what we've gotten into. Not so different from when we started out, making pictures in a few weeks, now is it?

JOAN. No, I suppose not...

BETTE. Or television for that matter.

JOAN. Oh, don't say that word. You know how I feel about the enemy.

BETTE. *(looking into the mirror at **JOAN**'s reflection)* Going out live, no rehearsal, fear of forgetting your lines! Well television is here to stay, let me tell you, so you better get used to it!

JOAN. Oh, Bette, no!

BETTE. But we don't have to completely surrender to it! There are still parts out there, and these are two of them!

JOAN. Well, I know. I was very aware of that fact when I discovered this property and brought it to you. *(With edge) Remember?*

BETTE. Look, you want this as much as I do, so I suggest we get on with it and make it work. Or do you want to do *What's my Line?* and *I Love Lucy* for the rest of your life?

JOAN. *(calming herself with more Pepsi before going towards* **BETTE** *with an outstretched hand, trying to find a glimmer of friendship between them)* Bless you for being so kind. I know we haven't always—

BETTE. I wasn't.

*(***BETTE** *exits, slamming the door behind her.* **JOAN***, agitated, perspiring again. Cross-fade to* **BETTE***'s dressing room. In time* **BETTE** *will complete her preparation.)*

BETTE. *(with satisfaction)* Ha! *That showed her!* As if I'm gonna sit back and let Aldrich and her call the shots; no way! *(Proudly)* I've always been a meddler, always wanted the finished product to be the best it could be, protected my work as I protected my family. Even with the odds stacked against me: bad directors, weak leading men, trite scripts!

(Revelling in the memory)

I've had more people tell me I've *exhausted* them over the years, than any other thing! *Exhausting! Just too much!* My inherited vitality, from my mother Ruthie, hasn't gotten any mellower as time's gone on. She looked to the future and so do I! Something Joan *of* Crawford should try, instead of harking back to the old days!

Anyway, enough about her. We've got another ten days shooting together which I'm not *wild* about, but, well, that's that. I need the money and I will say this, it's a damn good script. It's gonna take guts, but then I've never been afraid of taking risks. No guts, no glory.

(She applies the famous Baby Jane cupid's bow lips as **JOAN** *decants vodka into her Pepsi Cola bottle)*
At least she has stopped sending all those lousy gifts: flowers and chocolates and perfume for Christ's sake! Anybody would think she was a you-know-what-bian! I will say one thing for her though, give her her due: at least she's managed to take the pace up until now. Three weeks to shoot it! Youngsters of today couldn't handle that, right. But *her*, old enough to be their grandmother, here she is, hangin' on in there!

*(***JOAN*** is calmer with the help of Pepsi and deep breaths)*

JOAN. I owe it to my industry, to all my fans. I'm a giver, never a taker. *(Almost as a mantra of preparation as she paces back and forth)* I refuse to live in the past, I live for today, preparing for a glamorous, beautiful tomorrow.

Not knowing how that tomorrow ends is the chief ingredient of a happy life. I've lived a life my fans can only dream of, I have to enjoy it on their behalf. They put me where I am today, not MGM, not Warners, no: like my ankle straps, those fans have held me up one hell of a long time!

BETTE. I've always believed in taking on one's opponents, even if they are bigger!

I never relax my guard. Nevah! I can still remember being told I was a 'No good, sexless son-of-a-bitch!' Being asked 'Who'd wanna get you at the fade out?' Being called 'The Little Brown Wren' because I was so drab. I don't forget anything, the years of struggle, the years of stardom, the years of struggling to *keep* the stardom, and that's why I vow that the next picture I make for *father* Jack Warner, will be filmed on one of the 'A' list soundstages Bette Davis pictures helped to build for eighteen years in the thirties and forties and not in this dump!

(Calmer and very seriously) I always give the same piece of advice to any aspiring actress I think has a chance of making it. I tell them: not everybody can be your

friend. So *you* choose your enemies. And when you see them, you walk up to them and you say: 'You are my enemy!' And you know how you recognise your enemy?

(A beat) Anyone who gets in the way of your work!

(The telephone rings. She picks up the receiver angrily.)

Yes!... No, I don't need anythin'... Just let me know when it shows up. *(She slams the receiver down.)* Christ!

(JOAN's telephone rings. Lights up full on JOAN, perspiring heavily; her speech is punctuated by sips on her Pepsi. BETTE *continues to get ready/study her lines.)*

JOAN. Bob, Bob at last! Whatever happened to you, Bob? I was beginning to think you must have forgotten the way to my dressing room!... I haven't finished yet – where were you? I needed you... I said I haven't finished!

I've been in this business thirty-seven years, Bob, *eighteen* of them at Metro Goldwyn Mayer, the greatest studio in the world, and this is what happens! Now all of a sudden *she's* directing the picture and the schedule is changed! It throws me off balance. I have to build up to a scene; I can't just switch it on and off. No, sir! She does this to constantly undermine me! *Please don't interrupt me, Bob!* I've tried with her, tried to be her friend, why only the other day I gave her her daily gift: a box of her Phillip Morris cigarettes. I said to myself, 'Joan, at least she can use them.' And do you know what?... Not even a note of thanks!

*(*BETTE *lights a cigarette.)*

No, I haven't finished. You know, Bob, there was a time when I had hoped that she and I could have been more than friends. I've admired her for so long. I'd hoped that there might be something beautiful and tender there, especially at this point in our lives. You knew how much I'd wanted her for the part? You know the line 'we're sisters, we understand each—' *(Collecting herself, she has perhaps said too much. Snappily)* Yes, I know it is meant in a different context! Anyway, that is beside the point, just between her and I. But then she does this, the mother! And always belittling me on the set, sitting next to you behind the camera, and calling you at night to block the next day's shooting. I know, I call and call and you're *always* engaged!

(As JOAN*'s voice becomes louder* BETTE *rises and listens at the adjoining wall.)*

I'm as much an actress as she is. Just because my roots weren't in the damn, damn... *(Hunting for the word)*

BETTE. – legitimate?

JOAN. – legitimate, thank you, Bob, legitimate theatre! If she's so crazy about it why doesn't she stay there? Answer me that!

BETTE. 'Two queen bees in one hive' they say of us!

JOAN. You're wrong about that, Bob, we are not...

BETTE. *Very* wrong.

JOAN. ...the woman isn't a bee. She's a wasp! *(A beat)* But I should have been informed. That would have given me time to prepare for the scene, harness the intensity, hold it before I...

BETTE. *(chuckling, she moves from the wall)* Jesus!

(JOAN *listens to Bob.)*

JOAN. *(growing angrier)* ...She did what?... I can't believe it!... Well, I can of her. I see, I see, Bob. Well *I* wasn't privy to that, I'll have you know... No, no, she did not. I see, Bob. Well, even so, you should have checked with me... How dare she... I'm not some extra, I've got balls you know? You and I have worked together before, Bob, we have a history... Very well. Oh, I'll be ready. Don't you worry about that, Bob... *(Glancing at her watch, checking her schedule)* Yes, I'll be ready *and* prepared. You bet, I'll be prepared!

(She replaces the receiver)

That was very unprofessional of Bob, I trusted him. Just another of life's disappointments. In future I intend to make movies with beautiful, trustworthy people, not someone who goes behind my back to our director. And to think I found this damn property! I took it to her. Not that anyone has ever thanked me. *(Indignantly)* Not even a note!

(The following section is acted as a flashback, played under two spots. **JOAN** *carries a script.)*

BETTE. *(grudgingly. Rises)* I suppose though, I should give her some credit for finding the script.

I'd been appearing on Broadway, in Tennessee Williams' *Night of the Iguana*, when one night there was this oh-so dainty tap on my dressing room door. My dresser said that there was a Miss Joan Crawford to see me, and just as I was replying that I'd never heard of any Miss Joan Crawford, in she barges, looking like a hooker's mother!

JOAN. *(aside)* It was a very good production... Margaret Leighton was *wonderful* in the lead. And Bette was so pleased that someone had thought of her. I could see work was proving hard to come by!

BETTE. *(gruffly)* What do you want?

JOAN. I see you haven't mellowed.

BETTE. Who were you expecting? Doris Day?

JOAN. Dear Bette. Well I'll come straight to the point.

BETTE. Always best.

JOAN. I'm a businesswoman, I'm here on a mission; I have a job to do.

BETTE. I take it you were in tonight?

JOAN. Yes dear, but I didn't send a note round in case you got nervous.

BETTE. Ha! As if! So what do you want?

JOAN. Well, you know what a massive fan of yours I've always been.

BETTE. Are you really? How sweet.
JOAN. And that is why I come here tonight as a friend, a Good Samaritan.
BETTE. *(aside)* And I'd always thought she was 'that whore from MGM'. *(To* JOAN, *flatly)* Yea.
JOAN. *(aside)* So I handed her the script of *Whatever Happened to Baby Jane?*
BETTE. What the hell is this?
JOAN. It must be our next script. If you only make one more film in your life, make this one.
BETTE. You really are nuts aren't you?
JOAN. *(aside)* I must confess I was expecting a warmer welcome.
BETTE. What do we play?
JOAN. Sisters.
BETTE. Oh shit!

(JOAN *comes closer, looking past* BETTE, *blocking the door, to the photographs in* BETTE*'s dressing room.)*

JOAN. Only photographs of the children and your dogs, I see.
BETTE. To date I haven't met a dog I haven't liked. I can't say the same things about husbands!

(JOAN *laughs politely.)*

Anyway, I thought you'd given movies up to be Mrs. Pepsi Cola?
JOAN. *(a beat)* Alfred's dead. And I need the money.
BETTE. Well, we all need that, dear. Any Hollywood actor that says he is going back to the theatre to refine his craft is talking bullshit. Why do you think I'm here? I've got groceries to pay for.
JOAN. I know you're on your own and I know you're broke.
BETTE. And what has that got to do with you? *(Gesturing at the script)* Or what's-it-called, for that matter?
JOAN. *Whatever Happened to Baby Jane?*

BETTE. Yea.

JOAN. *(deadly earnest)* Absolutely everything.

(The two women look at each other. For a moment an understanding between them.)

BETTE. Everything?

JOAN. Everything.

(The lighting reverts to show we are back in the present.)

JOAN. *(aside)* Then she snatched the script off me and slammed the door in my face!

(JOAN turns and returns to her dressing table.)

BETTE. Hollywood being what it is – now run by the banks, who only respect money and youth – wanted to recast the picture with younger actresses, can you imagine! *(A beat. She begins to get into costume.)* Well, I suppose it has always been that way… money and youth!

JOAN. It was announced that Joan Crawford and Bette Davis would star in *Whatever Happened to Baby Jane?* – oh, I do beg her pardon: she did correct me (one of our longer conversations), that Bette Davis and Joan Crawford would appear in *Whatever Happened to Baby Jane?* Apparently her name always goes above the title and first. She gave a press conference stating as much. Such insecurities.

(JOAN changes into one of Blanche's 'monk' style costumes. Taking off the robe she will remove the blouse as well, replacing her mules for Blanche's flat pumps. BETTE changes into one of Jane's costumes.)

BETTE. *(in her underwear)* Who'd have thought it? Hollywood's oldest old bags together at last! I told some interviewer, just because we're over forty doesn't mean we're over the hill!

JOAN. I had to send her a note about that interview she gave saying we were washed up. I mean, really. *Washed up!* There are ways of getting a point across with a little diplomacy. I spoke to that same journalist. I told him, for it was a him, in this business one is constantly being reminded of one's age. I bet he'd never ask Cary Grant or James Stewart how old they were.

BETTE. *(dressing)* A star she is, yes, I'll give her that. But an actress? Nevah!

Joan has a very different temperament to mine. The things that are important to her, are very different to an actress, like myself. Even though she knows her lines and her marks and everyone else's like a pro. It's the attitude that really sticks in my craw. The plastic covers she insists on wrapping everything in, the shoulder pads that won't fit through the door, and the fucking Pepsi Cola dispensers on the set! She hides behind the Pepsi Cola Corporation, the same way she uses it to disguise the vodka!

Oh, oh, and because of germs, the only time I'm allowed to touch the bitch is when I slap her and even then she's using a double!

Knit one, pearl one – Ha! I bet she knits when she fucks!

JOAN. She makes me so mad! Her high-handed New England ways, schedule instead of skedule, biscuit for cookie! And the constant ribs about our age, my lack of education: so dismissive, it hurts! She fails to realise we are in this together. Oh, she says we should just get on with it, but she works alone, she always has.

The ingratitude!

BETTE. Anyway, I can handle her, I've had plenty of experience. Boy, have I fought some tricky characters over the years, though I must admit, most of them actors!

(She seats herself and puts on JANE'*s shoes, as the lights gradually dim.)*

I believe it's not natural for a man to become an actor. 'An actor is something less than a man, an actress *more* than a woman' Ha! I love that – had it engraved on my cigarette case, and damned right it is too!

Not that I include *her* in that actress category.

Can't believe I ended up married to an actor, something I swore I'd never do. *(A beat, very sincerely)* But I did. He was my last stab at matrimony, of that I am sure. No man will want me again, not for the reasons I want him to want me. Not for this old body. *(A beat)* They're tough, relationships, even tougher than I thought. Especially, when, like me, you're a loner – through instinct, not choice, instinct, however much you fight against it. Problem is that doesn't mean you want to be alone. And I did give the wife and mother bit the old college try. Loved being a wife and mother, my favourite parts.

Oh, but I have regrets, those people who say they have no regrets are talking crap. *Crap!*

(A beat) Anyway, skip it. Why ruin a good mood?

(Lights back up. There is a call for Miss Davis and Miss Crawford to be on set in five minutes. In time both rise, BETTE *minus the Jane wig, to examine themselves in the full length mirrors on the adjoining wall)*

JOAN. *(looking at herself frankly)* All my life I've wanted the Joan Crawford of this year to be only a building block for the Joan Crawford of next year. It took guts to do what I did, considering where I'd come from.

That's what I was showing Bob that day, as I had all my directors: all those years of struggle. Thank God my fans know how I've sweated to get here, and the price I have to pay to remain here. Bette is always making snide ribs about humble origins and the role of the casting couch in Hollywood. Well I'm not ashamed to say I welcomed a place on it. It sure beat the hard, cold floor!

BETTE. *(at the mirror)* The trouble with her is she has had no proper training. She was just a dancer when she started, then Norma Shearer's double. There are no shortcuts to success!

They say of me I am the only actress in Hollywood who has gotten to the top through sheer talent alone and not via the casting couch. Damned right! That's the difference between movie stars and actors.

(BETTE, *at the mirror, adds another layer of lipstick; in time she will put on the Jane wig*)

BETTE. I came to Hollywood from Broadway, the theatre! Closest she evah got was a seat in the stalls!

JOAN. She's a movie star just like the rest of us. If Broadway means so much to her why not do us all a favour and stay there?

BETTE. We all came West in those days. Talking pictures were the rage and theatre actors could talk!

Work became a lifelong love affair for me. In fact the only, truly rewarding love affair I've *evah* known. And I gave that love affair everything I possessed, and worked hard, harder than any other actress in Hollywood.

You see I wasn't some glamour puss, who could get by on her looks, no, I had nothing going in my favour, except talent.

(JOAN *undoes her hair net and primps her hair in the mirror; in time she will add a scarf to her neck*)

JOAN. I knew nothing about acting. I had a ten week contract: if I didn't prove myself in that short time I'd be discarded like so many others.

BETTE. I sometimes think I was a fool though to come to Hollywood, where they only understand platinum blondes and legs.

JOAN. The waxing, the colouring, the dyeing, the diets, the exercises. The sacrifices I made for my career and my fans.

It took balls. They understand and so should Bob. And so should she!

BETTE. *(to her reflection)* Great beauties do not make great actresses.

When you've poached egg eyes, limp hair, an Alice in Wonderland neck and bad posture, you just have to be good!

(JOAN *leaves the mirror and returns to the dressing table where she adds scent.*)

I don't give a fuzzy rat's ass what I look like!

(BETTE *cackles outrageously as Baby Jane.*)

JOAN. She had the nerve to say that if I was bothered about looking old on screen perhaps we should swap parts. As if I could play Jane, she's twice as ugly! *(Thoughtfully)* I just hope she doesn't try anything on the set... *(Nervously)* She might.

(BETTE *begins collecting her script, bag and cigarettes to head for the soundstage.* JOAN *picks up the telephone receiver and dials.*)

Hello Patreecia, would you be so kind as to get Miss Davis on the line for me... Yes, yes, I know we are wanted on the soundstage, but I don't think she has left yet. I just wanted to check something. Bless you, dear.

(*The telephone rings in* BETTE*'s dressing room, just as she is about to exit.*)

BETTE. *(barking into the receiver)* What?... Well, what does she want?... Well, put her through then, if you must... *(In her Baby Jane voice)* Yes?

JOAN. Hello? Bette? I just wanted to double check something... I was wondering...well, you...

(BETTE *isn't listening, but rather checking her make-up in the mirror.*)

Hello? Bette are you still there?

BETTE. Yes I'm here; you know we're needed on the goddamn set!

JOAN. *(hesitantly)* Yes, of course. I was wondering about—

BETTE. *(interrupting her angrily)* Jesus Christ, Joan, will you make it snappy!

JOAN. *(trying to make light of* **BETTE***'s rudeness. Gaily)* You know, Bette, I'm going to have to get myself a swear box if you keep on speaking to me like that! A nickel a—

BETTE. You do that, Joan. *(Vehemently)* And if you evah make it to the set I'll give you five bucks so you can go fuck youself!

(**BETTE** *slams down the receiver, then exits aggressively, slamming the door behind her. Lights black over her dressing room.*)

JOAN. Original she may be, a lady she ain't. Well I really did try. I *really* did.

(**JOAN***'s telephone rings.*)

(Into receiver) Hello, oh hello Bob, yes, yes I'm almost ready and we'll all be along in a moment... Yes, Bette did remind me about her back... of course I'll work with her... I'm a tough dame. I can handle it. See you in a moment. Thank you for your call. I appreciate it. Bless you, love and eternal trust.

(**JOAN** *replaces the receiver and reveals a heavy costumier box from under her dressing table. Opening the box* **JOAN** *takes out a weightlifters belt, attached to which are small weights. She holds it up to her waist, admiring her reflection. After a moment she opens her costume and begins to put it on. Once on she zips up her costume and checks her reflection.*)

It's marvellous to be a perfectionist, and to always remain a lady, not like that bitch Bette Davis.

(**JOAN** *exits, lights fade to black. Music*)

End of Act One

ACT TWO

(7:00 p.m. Darkness. Music fades out. Lights up very slowly on **BETTE***'s dressing room. Same as before. Voices off: muffled, unintelligible, anxious. Then clearer, closer, angry, raised. The sound of footsteps moving swiftly along the corridor. 'Miss Davis are you sure you will be OK?'/ 'Can we do anything for you... A doctor?')*

(Lights up. The door of **BETTE***'s dressing room is opened with force. Aldrich.* **'BETTE**, *I think she's afraid—')*

BETTE. *(cutting in)* Afraid of what? Afraid I'm gonna kick her fucking teeth in? She better be! We rehearsed this, Bob. She and I went over the damn scene together, then all of a sudden she wants to shoot in one take, no rehearsal, and the stupid bitch becomes the weight of King Kong!

(The voice of Robert Aldrich, off: 'Listen, Bette—')

If she'd been trained in the theatre she would know how to fake it! She's a fake in every other department!

(Aldrich, off: 'Please Bette, Joan is very distressed—')

Distressed? What the hell does she have to be distressed about?

(Aldrich, off: 'I believe she is in her john throwing up.')

Well, tell her to have a good crap, cause she's full of that too!

*(*****BETTE** *slams the door. In pain with acute back strain, she pulls the Baby Jane wig from her head.)*

(Furious) I say don't play it as if it were a fucking fairy tale, only to discover she weighs in like Johnny

Weismuller! I *had* to drop her, couldn't hold her a second longer!

And now, apparently, *I am informed,* she's crying... the bitch can piss tears!

(Grabbing the telephone she flops into the armchair, kicking off her shoes. Dialling an internal number. Into the receiver:)

Who is this?... Well, who the hell do you think it is? Get Jack Warner on the line...yes, yes, it is urgent! Put me through. *(After a short interval)* What do you mean he's just left for the weekend? It's Thursday! Tell that yella belly bastard he's a liar! Jesus!

(She slams down the receiver and lights a cigarette. She rises, pacing up and down, smoking furiously.)

If this were the forties I could have walked straight into Jack's office, but now...son of a bitch.

We're not even in a proper studio, snuck out on some back lot where Warners used to churn out their 'B' pictures. Like the trash!

(After a moment **JOAN** *enters her dressing room, first apparently tearful, a handkerchief to her face, then, gradually, she cannot hold the laughter in and is doubled up with hilarity. Voices off: 'Good night Miss Crawford' etc.* **BETTE***'s room remains lit.)*

JOAN. *(laughing helplessly as she removes the belt. In time she will get out of her costume)* Golly, what a weight! At one point I thought I'd ruptured something! She managed it in one take though, I have to hand it to her. But it had to be done – she had to be punished. God knows I've tried to be that woman's friend, for nearly thirty years — boy, have I tried. I've never known such resistance. They have all submitted in the past, yet every time I offered the hand of sisterhood... *(She enjoys her Pepsi)* Well, let's just say I see how she got all those awards: that wasn't acting at all, that was how she truly is!

Even at Jack Warner's phoney press launch (I wore a pastel shade of turquoise, beautiful when shot in soft focus) even then, Bette had to upstage me by wearing black.

I turned to Mr. Warner to thank him for this marvellous day. All he could say was, 'They tell me it will turn a profit – that's why I'm here.' I see now she inherited that trait of ruthlessness from her professional father – they're both monsters!

(Cross fade to **BETTE**. *Over the next section* **BETTE** *removes her costume and puts on her robe. She pours herself a small, neat scotch and lights another cigarette.* **JOAN** *tops up the vodka, from a flask, into her Pepsi Cola bottle.)*

BETTE. *(calmer, due to the drink. The light draws in. With humour)* I always say I play bitches because I am not a bitch; that is why Miss Crawford plays ladies! *(Laughs)*

JOAN. *(fastening her robe)* She's asked for more money up front, I do know that. Family trouble no doubt! We're both on percentage, but she gets less of the box office. I found that out. Well, if it wasn't for the jewels Alfred left me I'd be in the same boat. I need to keep working. Pepsi Cola took most of what Alfred made.

But I think I've been smart. I think I'm going to come out on top on this one, which, no doubt, will irritate the hell out of her. It took balls to negotiate that.

*(***BETTE**'s *telephone rings. She rushes to answer it.)*

BETTE. *(into the receiver)* Ah, Jack, I knew you'd… Oh Ruthie, Mother! *(Immediately she is a girl again)* Why are you calling the studio? I'll see you at home. Is everything alright? Is Bobby alright? Christ, what has she done now?… That's a relief… I know, Mother – it's just been rather a trying day, that's all… Oh please leave it until I get in, and then I'll sort it all… Well tell Bobby to leave it as well!… You know it will be too much for her. Jesus! I just wish you'd do as I ask you!… Well, Mother, I do, I'm sorry but… Oh Mother! I said

I was sorry, now tell you what, when this is all over we'll get that new fur I've been promising you. I know I said I couldn't afford it but…just let me finish, Ruthie darling. The three of us will have a spree again, the three musketeers, like we used to…but… Oh, oh I see. Well, I hope you charged it to me…you did…well that's fine… Alright, Mother, I'll see you at home.

(She slowly hangs up the receiver and downs her drink, lights dim.)

JOAN. *(choosing which outfit, from the many on the rail, to leave in and greet her fans in on leaving the studio. This is of major importance to* JOAN.*)* I heard her trying to get hold of Mr. Warner. She should have learnt that lesson. Hollywood fathers ultimately abandon their young. I learnt that from Papa Mayer.

(Lights up full on both dressing rooms, BETTE *cold creaming her face, her back still painful)*

BETTE. Without Daddy in my life Jack Warner became a surrogate father for me; and I wrestled with him, as I had wrestled with Daddy. I used to think being confrontational served me well… And like my real father, Jack cast me aside. He told me he never really liked my pictures, but as he told me, as long as they turned a profit… *(A beat)* Well, perhaps it was me he didn't like? Strange to be cast aside by both your fathers. Hard to take that.

(After a moment) Now where the hell is it? *(She picks up the receiver again, dials.)* This is Bette Davis… Has it arrived yet? I haven't heard anything from you… Yeah, just get on to it, will you?

(Replaces the receiver. Cross-fade to JOAN*)*

JOAN. Hollywood hasn't really changed since I first knew it in the twenties, when I was the baby of the lot; it's still full of fathers and adopted daughters.

I was lucky, though: without a father, I've not been fatherless; I had Papa Mayer and then, to some degree,

Papa Jack at Warners. Life has a way of compensating. I learnt from one what to expect from the other. A big fat zero.

(She begins to change into an elaborate multi-coloured outfit. Everything matches: hat, gloves, bag, ankle strap 'Pump me' shoes – these have a film of plastic over them.)

When it was my turn to leave MGM (my pictures had been making a loss for a number of years – I don't blame my fans, I blame the studio) Papa Mayer called me into his office: 'Now don't do anything foolish, Joan. Lay off the liquor and pills; you'll always be a daughter to me. Go with my blessing'.

So I quietly got up, and walked out.

When it ends...it is time to make a new start. And I had no option but to quit. He was a father who knew all about his daughter. All about her past.

All so easily accessed to punish me with.

BETTE. At least the studio had nothin' on me when I did leave. No blue movies that I hear still do the rounds at bachelor parties, like someone I could mention! *(She roars with laughter.)*

JOAN. *(a short pause)* You see we all have secrets. All of us. Every single one of us. Of course, if I hadn't made those films, that I oh-so bitterly regret today, I would never have got my first break, would never have earned my fare to Hollywood. I was just a goofy, stage-struck kid. *(Harshly)* But I learned, oh golly did I learn!

BETTE. *(a beat. Feeling better)* Anyway, let's just hope she can turn a profit. She and I have to! I really need a hit picture. Things have been see-sawing for me since the war ended. Back then it was fun to see posters proclaiming, 'Scare Hitler: send Bette Davis to the front!' But when the boys came home, they didn't want to be threatened at the pictures, especially by a female, and they stayed away in their droves.

No, this picture has got to make money, no question about it. As well as the kids to support (I can't expect a nickel from Gary) there's also the other two musketeers, Ruthie and Bobby, to think of. Bobby, the casualty of my parents' divorce… I would send her back east for treatment, to avoid the press finding out – it cost thousands. I'd visit her there and it was… horrible, just horrible.

I remember one visit I made – all the patients in the ward started to do Bette Davis impersonations! The cigarettes, the eyes, the…the… All that was missing was for one of them to start clipping out: *(Impersonating herself)* 'Petah! Petah! The lettah!' All of them except Bobby, silent for a year…just staring out the window.

Everyone bangs on about the weak needing to be looked after. But to my mind it is the strong who need the care for they do the caring!

Fame was my enemy and Bobby paid the price for it. I have to keep going for…for all our sakes. Be the monster for the three of us.

JOAN. You can skip childhood and education – I didn't have one. I learned everything staring into a lens. It clarifies everything beautifully, like a form of distillation. It forces you to travel alone.

You soon realise that no one is indispensable. Family, friends, husbands…nobody.

(JOAN *rises and exits, carrying a bottle of Pepsi and a package, still not completely attired to leave: minus hat, gloves, stole and jacket. Lights over her dressing room dim.*)

BETTE. Husbands, like relatives, invariably become needy… There were times when, what with Ruthie's overspending, Bobby's depressions and a husband to pay for, I felt I had three wives to support.

(A beat) I adore men though. Just never seem to bring the best out in them. Never been able to trust them, I suppose.

(There is a lady-like tap at **BETTE***'s door.)*

(Making up. Barking) Yes, what is it?

(JOAN *stands in the doorway.)*

JOAN. Oh, Bette. I just wanted to see how your back was.

(BETTE *ignores her and carries on at her mirror.)*

Well, may I come in, dear?

BETTE. If you must.

(JOAN *steps over the threshold.)*

JOAN. You sounded as if you'd ruptured something.

BETTE. Whatever made you think that?

JOAN. Well, the way you cried out in…in such pain.

BETTE. What'd ya do, tie weights to yourself?

JOAN. *(laughing politely)* Dear Bette, such a sense of humour.

BETTE. I'm fine, so you can close the door behind you.

(JOAN *lingers a moment, then steps further into the room)*

Oh Christ.

(JOAN *goes to the Baby Jane wig, all the time looking at* **BETTE** *in the dressing table mirror, making up and later brushing her hair out.)*

JOAN. *(a beat. Gesturing at the wig while looking at* **BETTE***)* So brave, to have to look like that.

BETTE. I presume you mean in the goddamn Baby Jane get up?

JOAN. *(a silvery laugh)* Why, of course. You must hate it though? I mean what did you have on today? It was all so tight, and the girdle strap showing and so grubby and unbecoming…

BETTE. Don't you evah believe in doing something because the character would do it? Look the way the character would look? I want to look like that.

JOAN. Well, of course you do, bless you, but I prefer to start inwards and...

BETTE. Oh, don't give me all that method crap! And while we're on the subject of inwards, do something about the padding – they're beginning to look like two hot air balloons!

JOAN. *(innocently)* What are, dear?

BETTE. You know very well. The falsies! (JOAN *looks blankly at* BETTE.) The inflatable boobs! You're meant to be a dying cripple.

JOAN. I don't know what you mean. Blanche deserves to be glamorous. I owe it to her.

BETTE. Then what the hell are you doing in *this* picture?

JOAN. *(flaring up)* Same as you: earning a buck!

BETTE. Ha, that's better! Show your teeth.

JOAN. Oh, I can do this type of movie; I won't make a goof of myself. So you don't have to worry. I proved I was a dramatic talent in the forties. Remember?

BETTE. Did you? No, I don't remember.

JOAN. I would just rather Hollywood invested in romantic—

BETTE. Well, even if it did, you could hardly expect them to cast you.

JOAN. I've often thought, I wonder if Bette sowed the seeds for all this unrest. I mean all those glorious performances in the thirties and forties, which we stood back and applauded, but on reflection: such anger, such discontent. You think I could be right?

(BETTE *looks daggers.*)

May I? (JOAN *takes a seat even though* BETTE *doesn't offer.*) Did you know, years ago, I used to roll your pictures after dinner parties...

BETTE. *(seething)* I see it didn't teach you anything.

JOAN. Now Bette, you have to admit I did win an Oscar.

BETTE. *Mildred Pierce* was an Oscar-proof part. Shirley Temple could have scraped an Oscar for that!

JOAN. Then why did you turn it down?

BETTE. Another picture directed by Mike Curtiz? Christ! No way!

JOAN. *(she smiles)* I suppose I can understand that. First day on the set he tore the dress from my back and yelled that he hated those son-of-a-bitch shoulder pads!

BETTE. That was his style.

JOAN. It was only when the dress was in shreds that he realised they were *my own shoulders!*

(BETTE relaxes a little and chuckles)

BETTE. Anyway, your one, for my two! *(A beat)* Though I must admit as a human being, you're a really great actress.

JOAN. *(after a moment's thought)* Bless you, Bette. *(Succinctly)* I'd like to add that being a great actress has made you a great human being.

BETTE. I'm well aware of my faults, Joan, but I'll just have to live with it, won't I. Collecting a third Oscar for Jane will be some source of recompense I'm sure. *(On her guard again)* Now what did you want?

JOAN. Oh, I agree. I'm sure the other nominees won't even bother turning up.

(JOAN expects a compliment back, but none is forthcoming.)

BETTE. Would show those bastards wouldn't it? Show Father Jack and the others. Trying to put me out to pasture. Huh!

JOAN. I was back at MGM recently. They made me feel like somebody's mother! There are no stars anymore.

BETTE. They don't exist. Just rows and rows of passive blondes.

JOAN. All made from the same cookie cutter.

BETTE. No guts! Debbie and Doris and—
JOAN. *(viciously)* That tramp Monroe.
BETTE. Now, don't speak ill of the dead.
JOAN. I wasn't, dear. I think it's a good thing that she's dead.
BETTE. Oh stop! She was a sweet girl, though anyone can wave their ass about.
JOAN. *(angrily. She rises and paces up and down.)* She killed the king! Filming *The Misfits*, she was always late on the set, and then when she did arrive, *drunk*, she didn't know her lines!
BETTE. *(under her breath)* Oh put a cork in it, will you!
JOAN. I mean how can you make a movie when you're loaded?

*(*BETTE *nearly chokes on her drink.)*

And poor Gable was kept waiting in the stifling heat, 108 degrees, while she got her shit together!

If only I had been on hand.
BETTE. And what would the latest Mrs. Gable have made of that?
JOAN. But of course Alfred would never have allowed—
BETTE. By the way, I was sorry to hear he had died.
JOAN. Though you couldn't say anything at the time?
BETTE. You wouldn't have wanted me to.
JOAN. *(a beat)* I suppose not. Well, thank you, dear, even if it is a tad behind skedule. It seemed unfair, losing him so soon after we married... Of course you lost one too, didn't you?
BETTE. *(recollects)* It was years ago.

(A beat) If he hadn't died, I expect I would have had to divorce him! *And* I wouldn't have had the children I have now.
JOAN. Your second husband, wasn't it?
BETTE. Possibly. Or have met Gary.
JOAN. But that's all over, isn't it?

BETTE. Oh Christ yes. Best thing I evah did, kicking that shit heel out. He was another man not man enough to be Mr. Bette Davis! I shall simply become an old lady living on a hill.

JOAN. You don't think you'll ever take another husband?

BETTE. No way! I'm zipping it all up!

(A beat as JOAN *digests this remark)*

JOAN. Alfred was very different of course. I found the one in him. I truly did. The name Steele suited him – he was such a rock. So different to be married to one of the world's most successful businessmen after all those actors. I made him the centre of my life. When he would return from work, I was well groomed, fragrant, feminine. With a bath run and a drink ready. He never saw a laundry bag, a dust cloth, a hair curler. I hope he never knew that such things existed!

BETTE. I should have married you! I could never find a man to do all that for me!

JOAN. After he died, I said to myself, 'Joan, why stay at home and mope? Pick yourself up and be the glamorous person you're supposed to be'. *(A beat)* That is the reason I'm working again.

BETTE. There are times when I wish I *was* a widow again, especially now that Gary is behaving like such a shit about the custody of Michael.

JOAN. Michael?

BETTE. Our son. My beautiful, blonde, American boy.

JOAN. But you had a dog called Mike. I remember seeing you with him – took him everywhere.

BETTE. Yeah, I know. I loved that dog.

JOAN. So you called your son after your dog?

BETTE. Yeah! It's a great name. And if Gary thinks he is gonna have him... *(She rises, angrily downing her drink.)* Well, I'll nail that yella belly drunk, you see if I don't!

JOAN. I never worked with Gary. Not sure I ever met him. I liked him as an actor...

BETTE. *(pouncing on the word) Exactly. An actor!* Didn't the career mean anything to him?

JOAN. With Alfred, I gave up for a little while. I thought he deserved it, and I, as a woman, wanted to do that for him, I—

BETTE. Oh, I could nevah do that! *(Looking into her empty glass)* Without my work I'm…well, nothing.

JOAN. Well, I'm certainly glad I did… At least we had that time building Pepsi Cola. A pillow is a lousy substitute for a man.

BETTE. And a man is a lousy substitute for a decent script!

JOAN. You really believe that?

BETTE. I do. My father was a shit; my sister married a shit; my four husbands were shits. You were lucky: another few years and he might have been a pain in the ass like Gary.

JOAN. No, I don't think so. Alfred was diff—

BETTE. I miss the fighting though, with Gary—

JOAN. You miss fighting?

BETTE. Sure I do! And the making up. He met me blow for blow, like none of my other husbands had.

JOAN. *(failing to understand* **BETTE***)* Men have all sorts of ways of hitting women, Bette, and not just the physical. You should know that, especially in Hollywood, dear. *(A beat)* Though it seems *our* adopted fathers are all departing, leaving us to fend for ourselves in this jungle.

BETTE. *(continuing getting ready to leave)* Well, Warner is still here only his mask has slipped. And remember, we left them and they soon replaced us!

JOAN. They will never actually replace *us.*
    At least, though, there is Grace Kelly: a beacon of beauty and charm in our dark future.

BETTE. *(adding another layer of lipstick)* And then the stupid bitch gets married and gives it all up! *Princess Grace!* Ha! Even you didn't manage that.

JOAN. But so glamorous!
BETTE. *(not being able to resist the jibe)* The second biggest hole in Hollywood!
JOAN. *(rising, furious)* Bette!
BETTE. *(holding up her hand to calm her down)* Alright, alright! Anyway, let's just hope I do scoop an Oscar for Jane, prove the old bags still have it in 'em, eh!
(She puts a hand on **JOAN**'s *arm, which placates* **JOAN** *for a moment.)*
Anyway, what *did* you actually want?
JOAN. *(thrown off guard for a moment. She sits again.)* Well, well, to see how your back was of course and...well...
BETTE. And, it is fine.
JOAN. And...
BETTE. Yes?
JOAN. *(producing the package)* Now, it's not what you think—
BETTE. Oh Christ not another gift!
JOAN. No, dear. See what I have here *(She unwraps the package producing a book)* The Lonely Life.
Such a sad title for a book...
BETTE. It means the loneliness of the artist's life. Anyway, what the hell are you doing with a copy of my autobiography?
JOAN. Well, I wanted you to sign it for me of course.
*(***BETTE*** sighs.)*
Was wondering if I get a mention –
BETTE. *(taking a pen. Dryly)* You don't!
(The lights dim. The sound of a projector running, incidental music creating an air of suspense. **BETTE** *can't think what to write.* **JOAN** *begins to look uncomfortably at* **BETTE***. Eventually* **BETTE** *writes a brief message, then with a malicious smile returns the book.)*
(Handing the book to **JOAN***)* There.

JOAN. *(nervously)* Bless you.

(BETTE *rises and moves slightly out of the pool of light, leaning against the door and playing with her bracelet. The tension rises as* JOAN *apprehensively looks at the closed book, not sure whether to open it.* BETTE *watches her.* JOAN *looks at* BETTE. *Music increases as she nervously brings herself to open the book. She reads the inscription. After which, like Blanche with the rat on the salver, she angrily pushes the book away from her onto the floor.* BETTE *roars with laughter like Baby Jane. Hand over her mouth, doubled up with hilarity, she totters out of the room. She totters against* JOAN*'s dressing room door and into* JOAN*'s room. The lighting etc. returns to normal.* JOAN, *furious at the insult, follows her into her own dressing room.*)

JOAN. 'Thanks for wanting my autograph, Bette Davis' Thanks for wanting my autograph! *How dare you write that!* Such arrogance! Thanks for wanting my autograph!

(BETTE *cackles.*)

BETTE. *(still laughing though growing angry by* JOAN*'s reaction)* I've gotta get out of here, so if there isn't anything else...

JOAN. I had a line in a movie once: 'Bad manners the infallible sign of genius'. In your case the two do not go hand in hand!

BETTE. *(suddenly aggressive)* Yes, I know the line. It was from one of the pictures intended for me! When I got back from maternity leave, my role, my line, until you got your grubby paws on the script!

JOAN. What nonsense, *Humoresque* was always intended to be a Joan Crawford vehicle.

BETTE. Bullshit! You're a liar, you always were! You even asked Jack Warner for my dressing room when I left. At least the son of a bitch had the good manners to refuse you that!

JOAN. I don't know what you mean. You're delusional. You've been drinking!

BETTE. Ha! You're jealous of me, and you've always been jealous of me. Just because you couldn't reach the top of the pile at MGM because there was Norma Shearer and then there was Garbo, and when they had finished, just when you thought you'd be top dog, in they flew, from London, England, because they couldn't find a decent actress on their own lot, Greer Garson! You couldn't get to the top there, so you thought you'd have a go at *my* studio.

JOAN. And you couldn't bear the thought of sharing your throne. The one thing, the one thing you feared most, came to pass. That another actress could be as great as you!

BETTE. Now who is being delusional!

JOAN. All I wanted was to be accepted at your studio, liked, even, but oh golly no, the Queen Bee just couldn't let that happen!

BETTE. Why the hell would I have done that? I didn't want you there.

JOAN. But they wanted me there. The Warner Bros. wanted me! Your box office gold was wearing thin. They wanted me instead of you!

BETTE. Oh get out, will you? You're beginning to sound like one of your phoney pictures.

JOAN. *(icily)* I'd love to, Bette dear, but it's rather difficult as we are in *my* dressing room!

BETTE. *(suddenly realizing)* Oh shoot! Well, before I go I will say this: you resent the fact that we have never been friends and yet why, why, why, would I befriend someone who tried to steal all that I had fought so hard to build up?

There will *nevah* be a friendship! And all this talk about reteaming us if this is a hit- well, you can forget it! No partnership, no way!

JOAN. Time will tell on that! You may find history remembers us differently. *(A beat)* I had hoped we could have been friends, you know...

BETTE. *(in the doorway. Sarcastically imitating the last scene of the film)* 'After all this time? You still want us to be friends?' Ha! Save it for the last scene will you; you're always mixing fantasy with real life!

(She exits, furious, slamming the door, and enters her own dressing room, heading for the Scotch bottle and a cigarette. The lights dim on **BETTE***'s dressing room as* **JOAN** *takes a deep breath and proceeds to sort furiously through her fan mail and autographed photos, placing them into ordered piles; all this is part of the process of filling the time before she must leave the studio.)*

JOAN. *(as she exhales)* Thank heavens for my Christian Science practitioner. She's a marvellous woman and the only fat person I tolerate in my life. *(She settles down to work.)* Now then... *(To herself as she writes)* 'Dear Margery, bless you, Joan Crawford. Dear Peggy, bless you, Joan Crawford...'

She is still so angry, so guarded...and defensive. Threatened, of course. She was like it in the forties and she's still like it today. The daughter is just as bad – she is a similar age to my twins, Cathy and Cindy.

Actresses should never have daughters. Of course I've been extremely lucky. I've been the exception, because I haven't been afraid of discipline.

Christina, my eldest, is even following in her Mommie's footsteps; I think we're going to hear a lot more from that young lady in the future, a lot.

Now then... 'Dear Phyllis, bless you, Joan Crawford... and dear Irving, bless you, Joan Crawford...'

(Cross-fade to **BETTE***, adding her jewellery, still worked up.)*

BETTE. It is times like this I see now how right Queen Elizabeth was – she ruled *alone!* *(A beat, reflecting on* *what she has said. Calming herself)* I've always had a great affinity with Good Queen Bess. A mother who would lose her head for her and a father who...well my dear! She had the ability to travel – *light.*

My mother always taught me, 'The universe is vast, Bette dear, and you are its centre', to which Daddy would reply, 'See all those stars up there? Now, Bette, remember how unimportant you are.' While Mother is still with me I *am* important. I'm still the most important person in someone's life. But when she goes...

(Cross-fade to **JOAN**'s *dressing room. She pats a large pile of A4 photographs.)*

JOAN. I sign up to ten thousand photographs a month. I don't begrudge it. This is Joan Crawford's applause and I've made so many beautiful pen pals, that even when alone I can never really be lonely. *(With emotion)* I so want to be liked.

(Cross-fade to **BETTE** *checking her watch)*

BETTE. I must get home to Mother – she'll be waiting. *Home.* Home can sometimes become somewhere you go, when you've nowhere else to go.

(A pause)

JOAN. I hate leaving the studio at night. When I was making a picture with Gable we would prepare for the next day's shooting together, clean our own dressing rooms, and then depart the studio to spend the evening making love. *(A beat)* And now he's gone...

I'd trade all my marriages, save the last, for one moment with Gable. Oh golly yes! Strange how when one marries one imagines that you'll be taken care of... Oh, it's beautiful in the beginning, but then... well, it never lasts. At least I had it with Alfred. It was all so beautiful with him. But the others? I soon realized they didn't actually want a wife at all. It was a mother they needed, and one with a pretty fat cheque book!

After Alfred's death, I was proud to sit on the Pepsi Cola board, in his memory. But after a while, I knew, and boy, did they made it clear, that I had to start pushing my own brand again, the only one I can rely on: Joan Crawford!

(Cross-fade to **BETTE**. **JOAN** *drinks)*

BETTE. Of course if I'd been smarter and married the love of my life, I'd have had an even greater career and not be alone today.

But I was an idiot.

The greatest man I evah met, and my finest director; no question about it, the love of my life. William Wyler.

Short, Jewish, with a toothy grin and the sort of eyes that bore into your soul.

I found his manner rather unprepossessing to start with, though. You see, I'm the kind of actress who needs some feedback from her director, I need to know he's happy with me. But after a few days on shooting *Jezebel*, our first picture together, well, nothing, *nothing*. I said to him, 'Mr. Wyler' (I'm not a first name kind of a girl) 'Mr. Wyler, I would like to know if you're happy with my performance so far.' The next day: *(Impersonating Wyler)* 'Miss Davis,' (He wasn't a first name kind of a boy) 'Miss Davis, that was marvellous.' And a little later, 'Miss Davis, that was wonderful.' *(Clapping hands)* 'Bravo!' By 11 a.m. I told him to skip it!

Brother, was he tough though. I felt he was trying to wear me out! He said I fidgeted too much, had too much energy: 'Keep your fingers still! Stop twitching!'

Well, I was putty in his hands. I always say, if he'd asked me to jump into the Hudson River, I would have.

His aloofness, at the beginning of shooting – being a Yankee I admired such reserve – masked a desire that, that…scorched me. I'd never felt so wanted, so… possessed.

(**BETTE** *rises to go to her handbag to retrieve her handkerchief and light a cigarette. The light widens to show* **JOAN** *listening at the adjoining wall. She hears the click of the handbag clasp and returns to her dressing room.*)

JOAN. *(almost vindictively)* She's still in there. I can hear her. She'll kid herself it is a mark of professionalism to be the last to leave and one of the first on the set each morning. I know all the tricks. She has nothing on me, of course; I once spent Christmas in my trailer to be ready to start shooting the day after – now that's being a professional.

BETTE. My first marriage was over in all but name. I felt lost, at sea, and then suddenly, this force, this whirlwind… well, it almost overtook me. The studio became my home, day and night. With love and work entwined, my life at last seemed complete. I would have a man who would take control of me, and I thought I was willing to let this great man do that. Not as Daddy had wanted to control me…but… Well, it terrified me.

JOAN. I'm quoted as saying that when asked if there is anything I would change in my life I always reply 'No! If I hadn't had the pain I wouldn't be me. And I like being me!' That's what Joan Crawford says, but, but you see Joan Crawford doesn't really exist. She was just a name picked out of a hat by the studio.

I often wonder what would the girl who was Lucille LeSueur say? Lucille LeSeuur, which sounded like sewer, so of course she had to go – yet my origins were in that name.

My daddy got out, Daddy left – they made him go, Mother and my brother. He couldn't stand it anymore. I don't blame him, just wish I'd had a similar option. *(A beat. Sadly)* Golly, I loved that man.

When I finally escaped, they followed me to Hollywood. Mother always at me to pay her speeding fines; cover her petty theft; pay off the charge cards. My brother came soon after: a drunk.

(As in Act One for 'The Letter' moment, the lighting changes to resemble film. Sound of a projector running)

When I took my place before the cameras for *Mildred Pierce*, I was told that the role would herald a departure for me. Bull! There wasn't anything I didn't know about serving food, scrubbing floors, mending clothes. The smell of grease and sweat and the hate a daughter can feel for her mother. It wasn't a departure at all. The part just brought me full circle. *Mildred Pierce*, Scene 43. Interior: Mildred's modest home. Veda brags to her mother of her deceit to obtain money. Mildred, appalled, asks Veda why does she want money so badly. The camera cuts back and forth between mother and daughter. Close up on Veda as she spits out words, words I'd said to my own mother.

'I want to get away from you and every rotten, stinking thing that makes me think of you! From your filth and your men and your liquor soaked breath; and this house like a pig pen and everything that smells of sweat!'

Mother screamed at me: *'Get out! Get out! Get out of this house, before I throw you into the street. Get out before…before I kill you!'*

And she would have. She was a whore, with a new 'uncle' for me every week, and I was glad when she died, glad, *and* my brother, drank himself into the ground. Glad, glad!

(A beat) There was no beauty you see and there must always be beauty and glamour.

*(She sits and sips Pepsi. The lighting returns to normal and the projector stops. Lights up on **BETTE**)*

BETTE. When Willie and I worked together for a third time, we were both pretty important people in Hollywood, and we clashed over my interpretation of the part,

quarrelled night and day, and I, 'Uppity New England Actress', walked off the set! Fool, *fool!*
By that time, I thought I knew it all, couldn't be taught I… *(Upset. Lights a cigarette)* I shouldn't do this. Looking back is relaxing one's vigil. I vowed I would never do it.

JOAN. *(calmer)* The last time I saw my daddy was on a film set. I was making a movie with the King, and there he stood, a tall, lean man, with hollows in his cheeks, bigger than mine: my daddy. He wanted to say something to me, but the words just wouldn't come out, and so we sat a moment, his hand tight in mine and I looked into his eyes, eyes that were like looking into my own, and it was a scene from a movie I never made.

Eventually he said: 'Baby, you're everything I'd hoped you would be' Just that; and it was oh, so gracious…so terribly fragile and gracious.

I was called back to the set, and when I turned to see him again, he was gone.

BETTE. I returned to the set and Willie and I finished the picture, barely speaking to the other, such did our work matter to each of us.

And to think it could have all been so different, I could have had it all… But I was proud, believed I was right, and he taught me a lesson.

While away from the shoot, furious at Willie's treatment t'ward me, exhausted by the constant rows and disagreements, hoarse from screaming at him, the son of a bitch! – a *letter* came from him. I ignore the damn thing, of course, think I'll torture him; make the bastard wait.

Two days later, I hear that fucking bitch Louella Parsons, spouting her crap over the airways, informing her listeners that *(impersonating Parsons)* 'Talented, clever William Wyler, has just gotten married to actress Margaret Tallichet! What a secretive man you are,

Willie! Congratulations!' *(Composing herself, blowing her nose)* Moral of the story? Open your fucking mail!

(She collects her things, ready to leave. Cross-fade to a circle of light over **JOAN***)*

JOAN. I can still remember dancing in the yard at the back of the laundry my mother embarrassed me by running. One day my foot landed on a shard of glass, hidden in the dirt. I can still see the dirt turning redder and redder. Mother was furious that I cost her a doctor. The doctor said I might always walk with a limp, but I proved him wrong, I proved that to myself – no way, I'd walk as straight as an arrow, right out of that hell forever, just like Daddy did. I'm a strong dame, I do not limp.

So when a director says to me, 'Would you be able to cry at this point, Miss Crawford?' I always answer, 'Why, of course, happy to oblige... Which eye?'

(Lights up full on both dressing rooms. Pause as both compose themselves, regaining control)

BETTE. Maybe we wouldn't have made it. Maybe I would have been too damn much for him too! Who knows? I love the idea of marriage, yet I'm always forgetting that the man has to be married to me! *(She chuckles. A beat, serious)* I think in time, though, one of us would have had to surrender...

Still, as long as I have my work I'll be fine. I survive because I am *tougher* than everybody else.

JOAN. *(rising to put on wrap, hat and shoes, she carries her gloves)* At least I have my career and my wonderful fans. They are my *survival*.

(Lights fade on **JOAN***'s dressing room as she exits.)*

BETTE. But, oh, to be thirty-five again! The perfect age. Anybody who believes life begins at forty is a fucking idiot!

Thank Christ I've played the women I've played. Other actresses wouldn't have taken those risks, wouldn't even

play a mother. But that is what being a proper actress is all about. And that has always been my maxim. I'm a working actress, plain and simple. An actress from New England. One whom people have learned to love. *(Suddenly with relish, pointing towards the other dressing room)* And that's why I'm not playing that silly bitch in the wheelchair! *(To the Jane wig)* Anyone could do that, but what I'm doing in this picture, *this, this part takes guts!*
I am living proof that the wheel that squeaks the loudest gets the grease!

(The telephone rings. She picks up the receiver.)

What? What?... It's here?... Christ... And Miss Crawford knows about it?

(She cackles with laughter, and cuts the speaker off, as she bangs down the receiver. There is a knock on **BETTE**'*s dressing room door.* **BETTE** *freezes.)*

JOAN. *(off)* Bette? Bette, are you in there?... Bette?

(Still **BETTE** *remains silent, though she flicks off some of the lights. After a moment* JOAN *enters, magnificently dressed to leave the studio and receive fans. She gasps as she sees* **BETTE** *sitting in an intimate pool of light.)*

BETTE. *(unapologetic)* Yea, I'm here, what do you want?

JOAN. *(still a little shocked)* Well, I think you know?

BETTE. *(looking her up and down. Chuckles)* Off home?

JOAN. Bette! Don't change the subject! I think you know why I'm here!

BETTE. Oh, really?

JOAN. *(getting angry, pointing to the set through the open door)* A Coca Cola dispenser has just been delivered onto the set!

BETTE. *(flatly)* Yea.

JOAN. Well?

BETTE. *(a beat)* I ordered it.

JOAN. Yes, I know, dear, oh, I know who ordered it.

BETTE. I prefer the taste.

JOAN. Now that I cannot allow, It's a stinker what you've done! And I just wanted you to know that I know. That's all. And I want it gone by tomorrow. I understand what you're trying to do, you see.

BETTE. *(turning her back on* **JOAN** *and adding scent to her hair)* Oh really?

JOAN. Oh, yes. I know what you're up to. You're not the only one to have fashioned a career playing bitches.

BETTE. Is that so? Well, if there isn't anything else, please don't let me keep you from your public.

*(***BETTE*** returns to what she was doing.* **JOAN** *hovers momentarily.)*

JOAN. By the way, I saw the rushes today…

BETTE. *(alert)* Oh?

JOAN. Of course I know you don't watch them, but—

BETTE. Can't stand the way I look, that's why. Now you know. I've never watched them, evah!

JOAN. *(knowingly)* Really? Well, I do, and I just thought I'd say that… that I think it's going to be a pretty fine picture.

BETTE. It damn well better be; no question, for both our asses. The first women's picture for years. Been one hell of a long time comin'!

JOAN. Dear Bette. Well I'm off home now. I'm still angry with you, don't ever forget that!

BETTE. Yeah, yeah. It's gotten late.

JOAN. Good night then. See you in the morning.

*(***BETTE*** busies herself at her dressing table.)*

Bette!

BETTE. Oh shit, good manners! Good night, Joan.

JOAN. Good night, Bette dear.

*(***JOAN*** exits smiling.)*

BETTE. *(pause as she waits for the sound of the door closing)* Gone! First to leave the set again, she's slipping! *(Rising, collecting her bag and battered script)* And now I can get out of here too. Need to call Bob when I get home, talk about tomorrow's shooting. And we need to change the schedule.

I think he's a genius though; he's actually coaxing an OK performance out of her. Of course it's all pretty obvious and one-dimensional, but then she's a pretty obvious and one-dimensional actress!

(She checks her watch) Must call him soon, he goes to bed so *damn* early, says the two of us exhaust him!

(Exiting) Need to run through that schedule, and tell him what a *cunt* she's been all day!

(The door slams. Blackout. Music)

The End

Lightning Source UK Ltd.
Milton Keynes UK
UKHW022314160223
417143UK00015B/479

9 780573 110535